THE
CHRISTMAS
CAROLING
SONGBOOK

ISBN-13: 978-1-4234-1419-3
ISBN-10: 1-4234-1419-5

HAL•LEONARD®
CORPORATION

7777 W. BLUEMOUND RD. P.O. BOX 13819 MILWAUKEE, WI 53213

Visit Hal Leonard Online at
www.halleonard.com

4

ALL THROUGH THE NIGHT

Welsh Folksong

Moderately

F   B♭   F   G   C   B♭   C7

Sleep, my Child, and peace at - tend Thee, all through the
While the moon, her watch is keep - ing, all through the
You, my God, a Babe of won - der, all through the

F   B♭   F   G   C

night; Guard - ian an - gels God will send Thee,
night; While the wea - ry world is sleep - ing,
night; Dreams you dream can't break from thun - der,

B♭   C7   F   Gm/C F/C Gm/C Am/C

all through the night; Soft the drows - y
all through the night; Through your dreams you're
all through the night; Chil - dren's dreams can -

B♭/C Am/C Gm/C F/C   Gm/C F/C C7 Dm Gm7   C7

hours are creep - ing, Hill and vale in slum - ber sleep - ing,
swift - ly steal - ing, Vi - sions of de - light re - veal - ing.
not be bro - ken; Life is but a love - ly to - ken.

F   B♭   F   G   C   B♭   C7   F

God His lov - ing vig - il keep - ing, all through the night.
Christ - mas time is so ap-peal - ing, all through the night.
Christ - mas should be soft - ly spo - ken, all through the night.

ANGELS WE HAVE HEARD ON HIGH

Traditional French Carol
Translated by JAMES CHADWICK

An - gels we have heard on high Sweet - ly sing - ing
Shep - herds, why this ju - bi - lee? Why your joy - ous
Come to Beth - le - hem and see Him whose birth the
See with - in a man - ger laid Je - sus, Lord of

o'er the plains, And the moun - tains in re - ply
strains pro - long? Say, what may the tid - ings be
an - gels sing. Come a - dore on bend - ed knee
heav'n and earth! Mar - y, Jo - seph, lend your aid;

Ech - o back their joy - ous strains.
Which in - spire your heav'n - ly song?
Christ the Lord, the new - born King.
With us sing our Sav - ior's birth.

Refrain

Glo -

- - - ri - a in ex - cel - sis

De - o, Glo - -

- ri - a in ex - cel - sis De - o.

AS WITH GLADNESS MEN OF OLD

Words by WILLIAM CHATTERTON DIX
Music by CONRAD KOCHER

As with glad - ness men of old Did the guid - ing
As with joy - ful steps they sped To that low - ly
As they of - fered gifts most rare At that man - ger
Ho - ly Je - sus, ev - 'ry day Keep us in the

star be - hold; As with joy they hailed its light,
man - ger bed, There to bend the knee be - fore
rude and bare, So may we with ho - ly joy,
nar - row way; And when earth - ly things are past,

Lead - ing on - ward, beam - ing bright; So, most gra - cious
Him whom heav'n and earth a - dore; So may we with
Pure and free from sin's al - loy, All our cost - liest
Bring our ran - somed souls at last Where they need no

Lord, may we Ev - er - more be led to Thee.
will - ing feet Ev - er seek Thy mer - cy seat.
trea - sures bring, Christ, to Thee, our heav'n - ly King.
star to guide, Where no clouds Thy glo - ry hide.

AULD LANG SYNE

Words by ROBERT BURNS
Traditional Scottish Melody

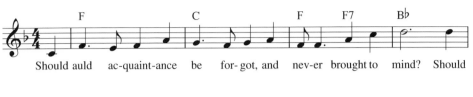

Should auld ac-quaint-ance be for-got, and nev-er brought to mind? Should

auld ac-quaint-ance be for-got and days of auld lang syne? For

auld ____ lang ____ syne, my dear, for auld ____ lang ____ syne, We'll

tak' a cup o' kind - ness yet, for ____ auld ____ lang ____ syne.

AWAY IN A MANGER

Traditional
Words by JOHN T. McFARLAND (v. 3)
Music by JAMES R. MURRAY

A - way in a man - ger, no crib for a bed, The
The cat - tle are low - ing, the Ba - by a - wakes, But
Be near me, Lord Je - sus, I ask Thee to stay Close

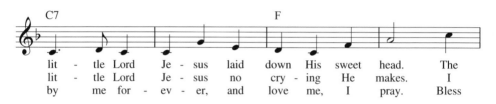

lit - tle Lord Je - sus laid down His sweet head. The
lit - tle Lord Je - sus no cry - ing He makes. I
by me for - ev - er, and love me, I pray. Bless

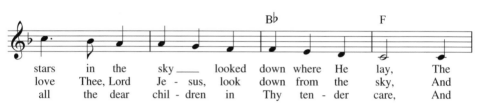

stars in the sky ___ looked down where He lay, The
love Thee, Lord Je - sus, look down from the sky, And
all the dear chil - dren in Thy ten - der care, And

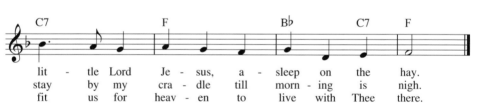

lit - tle Lord Je - sus, a - sleep on the hay.
stay by my cra - dle till morn - ing is nigh.
fit us for heav - en to live with Thee there.

BLUE CHRISTMAS

Words and Music by BILLY HAYES
and JAY JOHNSON

CAROL OF THE BELLS

Ukrainian Christmas Carol

Exuberantly

Hark to the bells, hark to the bells, tell - ing us all Je - sus is King!

Strong - ly they chime, sound with a rhyme, Christ - mas is here, wel - come the King!

Hark to the bells, hark to the bells, this is the day, day of the King!

Peal out the news o'er hill and dale, and 'round the town tell - ing the tale.

Hark to the bells, hark to the bells, tell - ing us all Je - sus is King!

Come, one and all____ hap - pi - ly sing ___ Songs of good will ___

O let them sing! Ring, _____ sil - v'ry bells,

Sing, _____ joy - ous bells! Strong-ly they chime, sound with a rhyme,

Christ-mas is here, wel-come the King! Hark to the bells, hark to the bells,

tell - ing us all Je - sus is King! Ring! Ring! _ bells. ___

CAROLING, CAROLING

Words by WIHLA HUTSON
Music by ALFRED BURT

With a lilt

Car - ol - ing, car - ol - ing, now we go; Christ - mas bells are
Car - ol - ing, car - ol - ing, thru the town; Christ - mas bells are

ring - ing! Car - ol - ing, car - ol - ing, thru the snow;
ring - ing! Car - ol - ing, car - ol - ing, up and down;

Christ - mas bells are ring - ing! Joy - ous voic - es
Christ - mas bells are ring - ing! Mark ye well the

sweet and clear, Sing the sad of heart to cheer.
song we sing, Glad - some tid - ings now we bring.

Ding, dong, ding, dong, Christ - mas bells are ring - ing!
Ding, dong, ding, dong, Christ - mas bells are ring - ing!

CHRIST WAS BORN ON CHRISTMAS DAY

Traditional

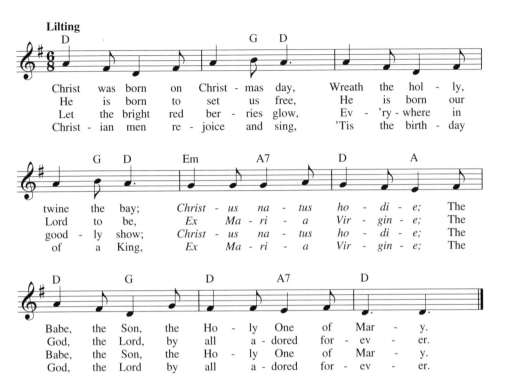

Lilting

Christ	was	born	on	Christ	- mas	day,	Wreath	the	hol	-	ly,
He	is	born	to	set	us	free,	He	is	born		our
Let	the bright	red	ber	- ries	glow,	Ev	- 'ry - where		in
Christ - ian	men	re	- joice	and	sing,	'Tis	the	birth	- day

twine	the	bay;	*Christ - us*	*na*	*- tus*	*ho*	*- di - e;*	The
Lord	to	be,	*Ex*	*Ma - ri*	*- a*	*Vir*	*- gin - e;*	The
good	- ly	show;	*Christ - us*	*na*	*- tus*	*ho*	*- di - e;*	The
of	a	King,	*Ex*	*Ma - ri*	*- a*	*Vir*	*- gin - e;*	The

Babe,	the	Son,	the	Ho	- ly	One	of	Mar	-	y.
God,	the	Lord,	by	all	a - dored	for	- ev	-	er.
Babe,	the	Son,	the	Ho	- ly	One	of	Mar	-	y.
God,	the	Lord	by	all	a - dored	for	- ev	-	er.

CHRISTMAS IS A-COMIN'

(May God Bless You)

Words and Music by
FRANK LUTHER

Moderately slow

When I'm feel - in' blue, An' when I'm feel - in' low,

Then I start to think a - bout the hap - pi - est man I know; He

does - n't mind the snow An' he does - n't mind the rain, But

all De - cem - ber you will hear him at your win - dow - pane, a -

sing in' a - gain an' a - gain an' a - gain an' a - gain an' a - gain an' a - gain.

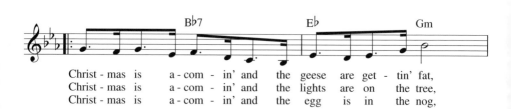

Christ - mas is a - com - in' and the geese are get - tin' fat,
Christ - mas is a - com - in' and the lights are on the tree,
Christ - mas is a - com - in' and the egg is in the nog,

Please to put a pen - ny in a poor man's hat. If you
How a - bout a tur - key leg for poor old me? If you
Please to let me sit a-round your old yule log. If you'd

have - n't got a pen - ny then a ha' pen - ny - 'll do, If you
have - n't got a tur - key leg a tur - key wing - 'll do, If you
rath - er I did - n't sit a-round to stand a-round - 'll do, If you'd

have - n't got a ha' pen - ny, may God bless you.
have - n't got a tur - key wing, may God bless you.
rath - er I did - n't stand a - round, may God bless you.

God bless you, gen - tle - men, God bless you, If you
God bless you, gen - tle - men, God bless you, If you
God bless you, gen - tle - men, God bless you, If you'd

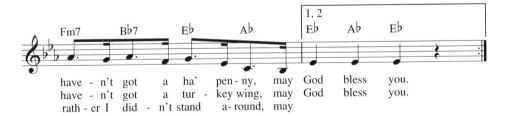

have - n't got a ha' pen - ny, may God bless you.
have - n't got a tur - key wing, may God bless you.
rath - er I did - n't stand a - round, may

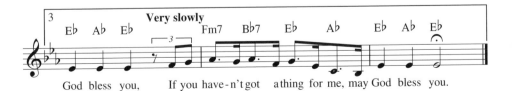

God bless you, If you have - n't got a thing for me, may God bless you.

THE CHRISTMAS SONG
(Chestnuts Roasting on an Open Fire)
Music and Lyric by MEL TORME
and ROBERT WELLS

Moderately

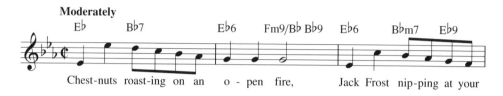

Chest-nuts roast-ing on an o - pen fire, Jack Frost nip-ping at your

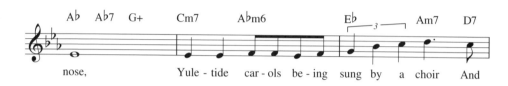

nose, Yule - tide car - ols be - ing sung by a choir And

folks dressed up like Es - ki - mos, Ev-'ry-bod-y knows a tur-key and some

mis - tle - toe ___ Help to make the sea - son bright.

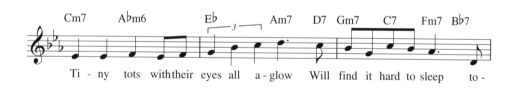

Ti - ny tots with their eyes all a - glow Will find it hard to sleep to-

night. They know that San - ta's on his way; He's load-ed

lots of toys and good-ies on his sleigh, And ev-'ry

moth-er's child _ is gon-na spy _____ To see if rein-deer _ real-ly know how to

fly. And so, I'm of-fer-ing this sim-ple phrase To

kids from one to nine-ty - two. Al - tho' it's been said man-y

times, man - y ways; "Mer - ry Christ - mas to you."

CHRISTMAS TIME IS HERE

from A CHARLIE BROWN CHRISTMAS™
Words by LEE MENDELSON
Music by VINCE GUARALDI

THE COVENTRY CAROL

Words by ROBERT CROO
Traditional English Melody

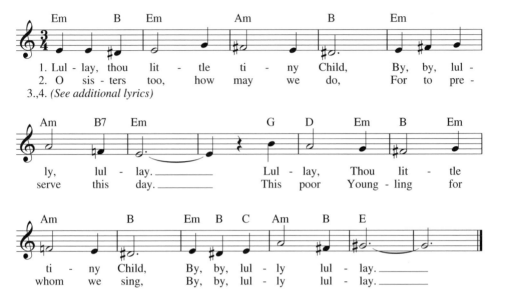

1. Lul - lay, thou lit - tle ti - ny Child, By, by, lul -
2. O sis - ters too, how may we do, For to pre -
3.,4. *(See additional lyrics)*

ly, lul - lay. _____ Lul - lay, Thou lit - tle
serve this day. _____ This poor Young - ling for

ti - ny Child, By, by, lul - ly lul - lay. _____
whom we sing, By, by, lul - ly lul - lay. _____

Additional lyrics

3. Herod, the King
In his raging,
Charged he hath this day.
His men of might,
In his own sight,
All young children to slay.

4. That woe is me,
Poor child for thee!
And ever morn and day,
For thy parting
Neither say nor sing
By, by, lully, lullay.

DECK THE HALL

Traditional Welsh Carol

Brightly

1. Deck the hall with boughs of hol - ly, Fa la la la la, la
'Tis the sea - son to be jol - ly, Fa la la la la, la

2.,3. *(See additional lyrics)*

la la la. Don we now our gay ap - par - rel,

Fa __ la la __ la la la la, Troll the an - cient

Yule - tide car - ol, Fa la la la la, la la la la.

Additional Lyrics

2. See the blazing Yule before us, Fa la la la la, la la la la.
   Strike the harp and join the chorus, Fa la la la la, la la la la.
   Follow me in merry measure, Fa la la la la la la.
   While I tell of Yuletide treasure, Fa la la la la, la la la la.

3. Fast away the old year passes, Fa la la la la, la la la la.
   Hail the new, ye lads and lasses, Fa la la la la, la la la la.
   Sing we joyous all together, Fa la la la la la la.
   Heedless of the wind and weather, Fa la la la la, la la la la.

DING DONG! MERRILY ON HIGH!

French Carol

Moderately

1. Ding dong! Mer - ri - ly on high in heav'n the bells are
2. E'en so here be - low, be - low, let stee - ple bells be
3. *(See additional lyrics)*

ring - ing. Ding dong! Ver - i - ly the sky is
swung - en, And i - o, i - o, i - o, by

riv'n with an - gel sing - ing.
priest and peo - ple sung - en.
Glo -

- - -

- - ri - a, Ho - san - na in ex - cel - sis!

Additional Lyrics

3. Pray you, dutifully prime your matin chime, ye ringers;
May you beautifully rime your evetime song, ye singers.

DO YOU HEAR WHAT I HEAR

Words and Music by NOEL REGNEY
and GLORIA SHAYNE

Moderately, with feeling

Said the night wind to the lit - tle lamb,
lit - tle lamb to the shep - herd boy,
shep - herd boy to the might - y king,
king to the peo - ple ev - 'ry - where,

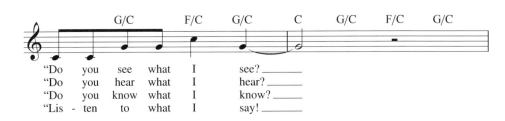

"Do you see what I see?
"Do you hear what I hear?
"Do you know what I know?
"Lis - ten to what I say!

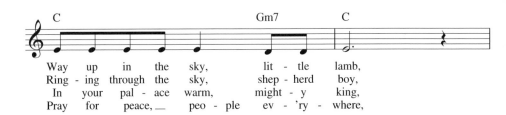

Way up in the sky, lit - tle lamb,
Ring - ing through the sky, shep - herd boy,
In your pal - ace warm, might - y king,
Pray for peace, — peo - ple ev - 'ry - where,

do you see what I see?
do you hear what I hear?
do you know what I know?
lis - ten to what I say!

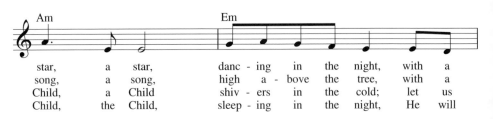

star, a star, danc - ing in the night, with a
song, a song, high a - bove the tree, with a
Child, a Child shiv - ers in the cold; let us
Child, the Child, sleep - ing in the night, He will

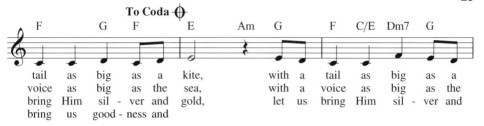

tail as big as a kite, with a tail as big as a
voice as big as the sea, with a voice as big as the
bring Him sil - ver and gold, let us bring Him sil - ver and
bring us good - ness and

kite." Said the
sea." Said the
gold." Said the

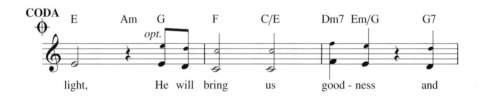

light, He will bring us good - ness and

light."

FELIZ NAVIDAD

Music and Lyrics by
JOSÉ FELICIANO

THE FIRST NOEL

17th Century English Carol
Music from W. Sandys' *Christmas Carols*

THE FRIENDLY BEASTS

Traditional English Carol

Moderately

1. Je - sus our broth - er kind and good Was
2. "I", said the don - key shag - gy and brown, "I
3.-6. *(See additional lyrics)*

hum - bly born in a sta - ble rude, And the
car - ried His moth - er up hill and down; I

friend - ly beasts a - round Him stood,
car - ried His moth - er to Beth - le - hem town."

Je - sus our broth - er kind and good.
"I", said the don - key, shag - gy and brown.

Additional lyrics

3. "I," said the cow all white and red,
   "I gave Him my manger for His bed;
   I gave Him my hay to pillow His head."
   "I," said the cow all white and red.

4. "I," said the sheep with the curly horn,
   "I gave Him my wool for His blanket warm;
   He wore my coat on Christmas morn."
   "I," said the sheep with the curly horn.

5. "I," said the dove from the rafters high,
   "I cooed Him to sleep that He would not cry;
   We cooed Him to sleep, my mate and I."
   "I," said the dove from the rafters high.

6. Thus every beast by some good spell,
   In the stable dark was glad to tell
   Of the gift he gave Emmanuel,
   The gift he gave Emmanuel.

FROM HEAVEN ABOVE TO EARTH I COME

Words and Music by
MARTIN LUTHER

From Heav - en high __ I come to you, To
This King is but __ a lit - tle child, His
Now let us all __ with songs of cheer, Fol -

bring you tid - ings __ good and true. Good tid - ings of __ great
moth - er bless - ed __ Mar - y mild. His cra - dle is __ but
low the shep - herds and draw near, To find this won - drous

joy I bring, To you this night is __ born __ a King.
now a stall, Yet He brings joy and __ peace __ to all.
gift of Heav'n, The bless - ed Christ whom __ God __ hath giv'n.

FROSTY THE SNOW MAN

Words and Music by STEVE NELSON
and JACK ROLLINS

found. / cop.   For / And he   when / on - ly   they / paused   placed / a   it / mo - ment   on / when ___   his /   head / he   he be- / he

gan / heard   to / him   dance / hol - ler,   a - / "Stop!"   round. / For   Oh, /   Frost - y / Frost - y   The / The

Snow / Snow   Man / Man   was / had   a - / to   live / hur - ry   as / on   he / his   could / way, ___   be, ___ /   And the / But he

chil - dren / waved good - bye   say / say - in',   he could laugh and / "Don't you   play ___ / cry, ___   just the / I'll be   same / back   as / a - gain   you / some-   and

me. / day."   Thump-et - y   thump thump,   thump-et - y   thump thump.

Look   at   Frost - y   go.   Thump - et - y   thump thump,

thump-et - y   thump thump.   O - ver   the   hills   of   snow.

FUM, FUM, FUM

Traditional Catalonian Carol

GO, TELL IT ON THE MOUNTAIN

African-American Spiritual
Verses by JOHN W. WORK, JR.

Go, tell it on the moun - tain, O - ver the hills and
ev - 'ry - where; Go, tell it on the moun - tain That
Je - sus Christ is born.

Last time Fine

1. While shep - herds kept their
2. The shep - herds feared and
3. Down in a low - ly

watch - ing O'er si - lent flocks by night, Be -
trem - bled When lo! a - bove the earth Rang
man - ger The hum - ble Christ was born, And

hold, through-out the heav - ens There shone a ho - ly light. ____
out the an - gel cho - rus That hailed our Sav - ior's birth. ____
God sent us sal - va - tion That bless - ed Christ-mas morn. ____

GOD REST YE MERRY, GENTLEMEN

19th Century English Carol

Brightly

God rest ye mer - ry, gen - tle - men, Let noth - ing you dis -
In Beth - le - hem, in Jew - ry, This bless - ed Babe was
From God our Heav'n - ly Fa - ther, A bless - ed An - gel

may, Re - mem - ber Christ our Sav - iour Was
born, And laid with - in a man - ger, Up -
came; And un - to cer - tain Shep - herds, Brought

born on Christ - mas Day, To save us all from
on this bless - ed morn; That which His Moth - er
tid - ings of the same; How that in Beth - le -

Sa - tan's pow'r, When we were gone a - stray;
Mar - y, Did noth - ing take in scorn,   O _____
hem was born The Son of God by Name.

Refrain

tid - ings of com - fort and joy, com - fort and

joy, O _____ tid - ings of com - fort and joy.

Copyright © 2006 by HAL LEONARD CORPORATION

GOOD CHRISTIAN MEN, REJOICE

14th Century Latin Text
Translated by JOHN MASON NEALE
14th Century German Melody

Good Chris - tian men, re - joice, _____ With heart and soul and
Good Chris - tian men, re - joice, _____ With heart and soul and
Good Chris - tian men, re - joice, _____ With heart and soul and

voice; _____ Give ye heed to what we say: News! News!
voice; _____ Now ye hear of end - less bliss; Joy! Joy!
voice; _____ Now ye need not fear the grave; Peace! Peace!

Je - sus Christ is born to - day! Ox and ass be -
Je - sus Christ was born for this! He hath ope'd the
Je - sus Christ was born to save! Calls you one and

fore Him bow, And He is in the man - ger now;
heav'n - ly door, And man is bless - ed ev - er - more.
calls you all, To gain His ev - er - last - ing hall.

Christ is born to - day! _____ Christ is born to - day!
Christ was born for this! _____ Christ was born for this!
Christ was born to save! _____ Christ was born to save!

GOOD KING WENCESLAS

Words by JOHN M. NEALE
Music from *Piae Cantiones*

1. Good King Wen - ces - las looked out On the feast of
2. "Hith - er, page, and stand by me, If thou know'st it,
3.-5. *(See additional lyrics)*

Ste - phen, When the snow lay 'round a - bout, Deep, and crisp, and
tell - ing, Yon - der pea - sant, who is he? Where and what his

e - ven; Bright - ly shone the moon that night,
dwell - ing?" "Sire, he lives a good league hence,

Though the frost was cru - el, When a poor man
Un - der - neath the moun - tain, Right a - gainst the

came in sight, Gath -'ring win - ter fu - el.
for - est fence, By Saint Ag - nes' foun - tain."

Additional Lyrics

3. "Bring me flesh, and bring me wine,
   bring me pine-logs hither;
Thou and I will see him dine,
   when we bear them thither."
Page and monarch, forth they went,
   forth they went together;
Through the rude wind's wild lament
   and the bitter weather.

4. "Sire, the night is darker now,
   and the wind blows stronger;
Fails me heart, I know not how;
   I can go no longer."
"Mark my footsteps, good my page;
   tread thou in them boldly;
Thou shalt find the winter's rage
   freeze thy blood less coldly."

5. In his master's steps he trod,
   where the snow lay dinted;
Heat was in the very sod
   which the saint had printed.
Therefore, Christian men, be sure,
   wealth or rank possessing,
Ye who now will bless the poor,
   shall yourselves find blessing.

HAPPY HOLIDAY

from the Motion Picture Irving Berlin's HOLIDAY INN
Words and Music by
IRVING BERLIN

HARK! THE HERALD ANGELS SING

Words by CHARLES WESLEY
Altered by GEORGE WHITEFIELD
Music by FELIX MENDELSSOHN-BARTHOLDY
Arranged by William H. Cummings

Moderately

Hark! The her - ald an - gels sing. __ Glo - ry to the
Christ, by high - est heav'n a - dored, __ Christ, the ev - er -
Hail, the heav'n - born Prince of Peace! __ Hail, the Son of

new - born King; Peace on earth, and mer - cy mild. __
last - ing Lord; Late in time be - hold Him come, __
Right - eous - ness! Light and life to all He brings, __

God and sin - ners rec - on - ciled! Joy - ful all ye
Off - spring of the vir - gin's womb. Veil'd in flesh the
Ris'n with heal - ing in His wings. Mild He lays His

na - tions, rise, __ Join the tri - umph of the skies; __
God - head see: __ Hail th'In - car - nate De - i - ty, __
glo - ry by, __ Born that man no more may die, __

With th'an - gel - ic host pro-claim, Christ is __ born in Beth - le - hem.)
Pleased as Man with man to dwell, Je - sus __ our Em - man - u - el! }
Born to raise the sons of earth, Born to __ give them sec - ond birth.)

Hark! The her - ald an - gels sing, Glo - ry __ to the new-born King.

HERE COMES SANTA CLAUS
(Right Down Santa Claus Lane)

Words and Music by GENE AUTRY
and OAKLEY HALDEMAN

HERE WE COME A-WASSAILING

Traditional

Gaily

Here we come a-was-sail-ing A-mong the leaves so green;

Here we come a wan-d'ring so fair___ to be seen; Love and

joy come to you, And to you your was-sail

too; And God bless you, and send___ you a Hap-py New

Year, And God send you a Hap-py New Year.___

THE HOLLY AND THE IVY

18th Century English Carol

1.,6. The hol - ly and the i - vy, when they are both full grown, of ___
2. The hol - ly bears a blos - som, as white as lil - y flow'r, and ___
3. The hol - ly bears a ber - ry, as red as an - y blood, and ___
4. The hol - ly bears a prick - le, as sharp as an - y thorn, and ___
5. The hol - ly bears a bark, ___ as bit - ter as an - y gall, and ___

Refrain

all the trees that are in the wood, the ___ hol - ly bears the crown.
Mar - y bore sweet ___ Je - sus Christ, to ___ be our sweet Sav - iour.
Mar - y bore sweet ___ Je - sus Christ, to ___ do poor sin - ners good.
Mar - y bore sweet ___ Je - sus Christ on ___ Christ-mas day in the morn.
Mar - y bore sweet ___ Je - sus Christ for ___ to re - deem us all.

The

ris - ing of the sun ___ and the run - ning of the deer, the ___

play - ing of the mer - ry or - gan, sweet sing - ing in the choir.

A HOLLY JOLLY CHRISTMAS

Music and Lyrics by
JOHNNY MARKS

Moderately bright

Have a hol - ly jol - ly Christ-mas, it's the best time of the year. _
hol - ly jol - ly Christ-mas, and when you walk down the street _

_ I don't know if there'll be snow but have a cup of cheer. _
_ Say hel - lo to friends you know and

_ Have a ev - 'ry - one you meet. Oh, ho, the

mis - tle - toe hung where you can see. Some - bod - y

waits for you, kiss her once for me. Have a hol - ly jol - ly

Christ-mas, and in case you did - n't hear, _ oh, by gol-ly, have a

hol - ly jol - ly Christ - mas _ this year. _

I HEARD THE BELLS ON CHRISTMAS DAY

Words by HENRY WADSWORTH LONGFELLOW
Adapted by JOHNNY MARKS
Music by JOHNNY MARKS

(There's No Place Like)
HOME FOR THE HOLIDAYS
Words by AL STILLMAN
Music by ROBERT ALLEN

Oh, there's no place like home for the hol - i - days; _____ 'Cause no

mat - ter how far a - way you roam, _____ When you

pine for the sun - shine of a friend - ly gaze, _____ for the

hol - i - days you can't beat home, sweet home. I met a

man who lives in Ten - nes - see and he was head - in' for Penn - syl -

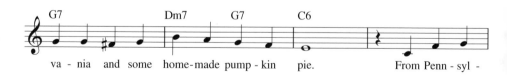

va - nia and some home-made pump - kin pie. From Penn - syl -

I SAW MOMMY KISSING SANTA CLAUS

Words and Music by
TOMMIE CONNOR

I WONDER AS I WANDER

By JOHN JACOB NILES

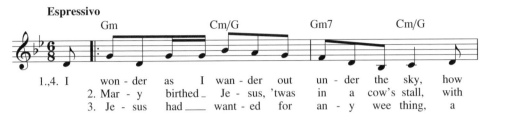

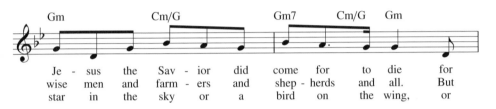

1.,4. I won - der as I wan - der out un - der the sky, how
2. Mar - y birthed _ Je - sus, 'twas in a cow's stall, with
3. Je - sus had ___ want - ed for an - y wee thing, a

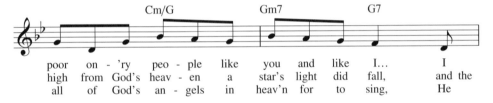

Je - sus the Sav - ior did come for to die for
wise men and farm - ers and shep - herds and all. But
star in the sky or a bird on the wing, or

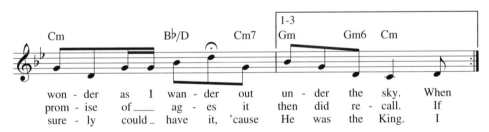

poor on - 'ry peo - ple like you and like I... I
high from God's heav - en a star's light did fall, and the
all of God's an - gels in heav'n for to sing, He

won - der as I wan - der out un - der the sky. When
prom - ise of ___ ag - es it then did re - call. If
sure - ly could _ have it, 'cause He was the King. I

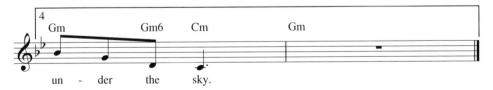

un - der the sky.

I'LL BE HOME FOR CHRISTMAS

Words and Music by KIM GANNON
and WALTER KENT

IT CAME UPON THE MIDNIGHT CLEAR

Words by EDMUND HAMILTON SEARS
Music by RICHARD STORRS WILLIS

IT MUST HAVE BEEN THE MISTLETOE
(Our First Christmas)
By JUSTIN WILDE
and DOUG KONECKY

IT'S BEGINNING TO LOOK LIKE CHRISTMAS

By MEREDITH WILLSON

It's be - gin-ning to look a lot like Christ - mas,

Ev - 'ry-where you go; { Take a look in the five and ten,
{ There's a tree in the grand ho - tel,

glis - ten-ing once a - gain, with can - dy canes and sil - ver lanes a -
one in the park as well, the stur - dy kind that does - n't mind the

glow. ____ }
snow. ____ } It's be - gin-ning to look a lot like

Christ - mas, { toys in ev - 'ry store, But the
{ soon the bells will start, And the

pret - ti - est sight to see is the hol - ly that will be on your
thing that will make them ring is the car - ol that you sing right with-

own front door. ____ A pair of
in your heart. ____

hop - a - long boots and a pis-tol that shoots is the wish of Bar-ney and Ben;

Dolls that will talk and will go for a walk is the hope of Jan - ice and Jen;   And

Mom   and Dad   can hard - ly wait   for school   to start   a - gain.   It's   be -

JINGLE-BELL ROCK

Words and Music by JOE BEAL
and JIM BOOTHE

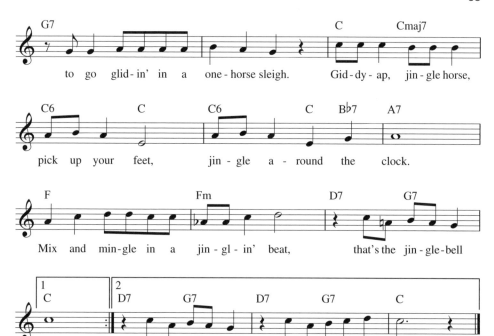

to go glid-in' in a one-horse sleigh. Gid-dy-ap, jin-gle horse,

pick up your feet, jin-gle a-round the clock.

Mix and min-gle in a jin-gl-in' beat, that's the jin-gle-bell

rock. that's the jin-gle-bell, that's the jin-gle-bell rock.

JINGLE BELLS

Words and Music by
J. PIERPONT

Brightly

Dash - ing thru the snow, In a one - horse o - pen sleigh,
Bells on bob - tail ring, _____ Mak - ing spir - its bright, what

O'er the fields we go, Laugh - ing all the way.
fun it is to

ride and sing a sleigh - ing song to - night. Jin - gle bells,

Jin - gle bells, Jin - gle all the way! Oh, what fun it

is to ride in a one - horse o - pen sleigh! Oh, one - horse o - pen sleigh.

JOLLY OLD ST. NICHOLAS

Traditional 19th Century American Carol

Moderately

Bb · F7 · Gm · Dm

Jol - ly old Saint Nich - o - las, Lean your ear this way!
When the clock is strik - ing twelve, When I'm fast a - sleep,
John - ny wants a pair of skates; Su - sy wants a sled;

Eb · Bb · F7

Don't you tell a sin - gle soul What I'm going to say;
Down the chim - ney broad and black, With your pack you'll creep;
Nel - lie wants a pic - ture book, Yel - low, blue and red;

Bb · F7 · Gm · Dm

Christ - mas Eve is com - ing soon; Now you dear old man,
All the stock - ings you will find Hang - ing in a row;
Now I think I'll leave to you What to give the rest;

Eb · Bb · F7 · Bb

Whis - per what you'll bring to me; Tell me if you can.
Mine will be the short - est one, You'll be sure to know.
Choose for me, dear San - ta Claus, You will know the best.

JOY TO THE WORLD

Words by ISAAC WATTS
Music by GEORGE FRIDERIC HANDEL
Arranged by LOWELL MASON

Brightly

Joy	to	the	world!	The	Lord	is	come;	Let
Joy	to	the	world!	The	Sav -	ior	reigns;	Let
No	more	let	sin	and	sor -	row	grow,	Nor
He	rules	the	world	with	truth	and	grace,	And

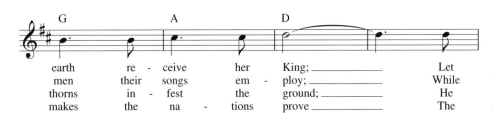

earth	re -	ceive	her	King; _____		Let
men	their	songs	em -	ploy; _____		While
thorns	in -	fest	the	ground; _____		He
makes	the	na -	tions	prove _____		The

ev -	'ry _____	heart _____	pre - pare _____	Him _____	room, _____	And
fields _____	and _____	floods, _____	rocks, hills _____	and _____	plains, _____	Re -
comes _____	to _____	make _____	His bless -	ings _____	flow, _____	Far
glo -	ries _____	of _____	His right -	eous -	ness, _____	And

heav'n and na - ture _____	sing,	And _ heav'n and na - ture _____	sing,	And _
peat the sound - ing _____	joy,	Re - peat the sound - ing _____	joy,	Re -
as the curse is _____	found,	Far _ as the curse is _____	found,	Far _
won - ders of His _____	love,	And _ won - ders of His _____	love,	And _

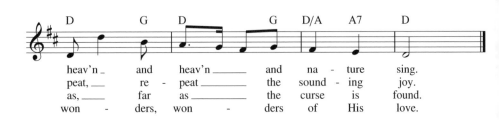

heav'n _	and	heav'n _____	and	na - ture	sing.
peat, _____	re -	peat _____	the	sound - ing	joy.
as, _____	far	as _____	the	curse	is	found.
won -	ders,	won -	ders	of	His	love.

LET IT SNOW! LET IT SNOW! LET IT SNOW!

Words by SAMMY CAHN
Music by JULE STYNE

LITTLE SAINT NICK

Words and Music by BRIAN WILSON
and MIKE LOVE

Moderately fast

Well, _ way up north where the air gets cold, _ there's a
lit - tle bob - sled, we call it Old Saint Nick, _ but she'll
haul-in' through the snow at a fright-'nin' speed _ with a

tale a - bout Christ-mas that you've all been told. _ And a
walk a to - bog - gan with a four - speed stick. _ She's
half a doz-en deer _ with _ Ru - dy to lead. He's

real fa - mous cat all dressed up in red, _ and he
can - dy ap - ple red with a ski for a wheel, and when
got - ta wear his gog - gles 'cause the snow real - ly flies, and he's

spends the whole _ year work - in' out on his sled. _
San - ta hits the gas, man, just watch her _ peel. _ } It's the
cruis - in' ev - 'ry pad with a lit - tle sur - prise. _

Lit - tle Saint Nick. (Lit - tle Saint Nick.) _ It's the

To Coda ⊕

1
Lit-tle Saint Nick. (Lit-tle Saint Nick.) _ Just a

2
Saint Nick.)

Run, run, rein - deer. _____ Run, run, rein - deer.

Oh. _____ Run, run, rein - deer. _____

Run, run, rein - deer. He don't miss no one. And

CODA

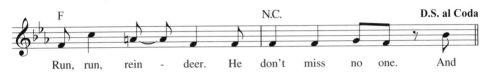

Lit - tle Saint Nick. (Lit - tle Saint Nick.) Ah, _____

Repeat and Fade

Mer - ry Christ- mas, Saint __ Nick. _____ Ah, _____
(Christ - mas comes this time each year.) _

A MARSHMALLOW WORLD

Words by CARL SIGMAN
Music by PETER DE ROSE

With motion

It's a marsh - mal - low world in the win - ter _____ When the
snow comes to cov - er the ground. It's the time for play, _ it's a
whipped cream day, _ I wait for it the whole year 'round. Those are
marsh - mal - low clouds be - ing friend-ly _____ in the arms of the ev - er-green
trees. And the sun is red __ Like a pump - kin head, _ It's
shin - ing so your nose won't freeze. The world is your snow - ball;
See how it grows. That's how it goes when - ev - er it snows. The

world is your snow - ball just for a song; get out and roll it a -

long. It's a yum - yum - my world made for sweet - hearts; ____ Take a

walk with your fa - vor - ite girl. It's a sug - ar date; _ what if spring is late? _ In

win - ter it's a marsh - mal - low world. ____ It's a world.

MERRY CHRISTMAS, DARLING

Words and Music by RICHARD CARPENTER
and FRANK POOLER

hol - i - day when I'm near to you. The __

lights on my tree I wish you could see, I wish it ev - 'ry

day. The logs on the fire _____ fill me with de - sire

to see you and to __ say that I wish you mer - ry

Christ-mas, hap-py New Year too. I've just one wish on this

Christ-mas Eve; I wish I were with you. The __

I wish I were with you. I wish I were with you.

MISTER SANTA

Words and Music by
PAT BALLARD

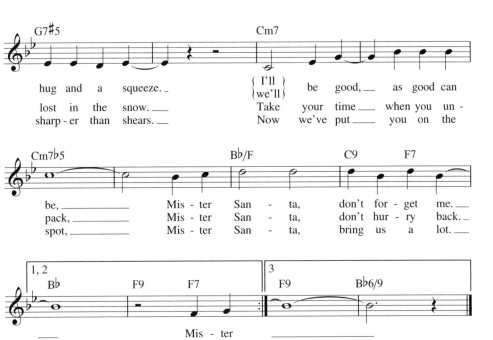

G7#5

hug and a squeeze. _
lost in the snow. ___
sharp - er than shears. ___

Cm7

{ I'll }
{ we'll } be good, ___ as good can
Take your time ___ when you un -
Now we've put ___ you on the

Cm7b5

be, ___
pack, ___
spot, ___

Bb/F

Mis - ter San - ta,
Mis - ter San - ta,
Mis - ter San - ta,

C9   **F7**

don't for - get me. ___
don't hur - ry back. _
bring us a lot. ___

1, 2

Bb   **F9**   **F7**

___
___

Mis - ter
Mis - ter

3

F9   **Bb6/9**

MISTLETOE AND HOLLY

Words and Music by FRANK SINATRA,
DOK STANFORD and HENRY W. SANICOLA

O CHRISTMAS TREE

Traditional German Carol

O Christ-mas tree! O Christ-mas tree, You stand in ver - dant

beau - ty! O Christ - mas tree! O Christ - mas tree, You

stand in ver - dant beau - ty! Your boughs are green in

sum-mer's glow, And do not fade in win - ter's snow. O

Christ-mas tree! O Christ-mas tree, You stand in ver - dant beau - ty!

THE MOST WONDERFUL TIME OF THE YEAR

Words and Music by EDDIE POLA
and GEORGE WYLE

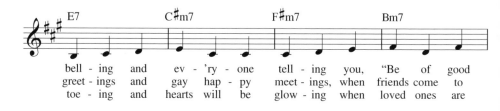

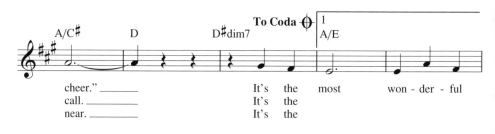

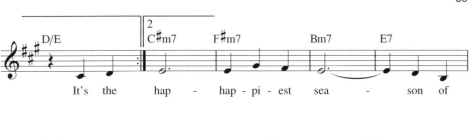

It's the hap - hap - pi - est sea - son of

all. _____ There'll be par - ties for

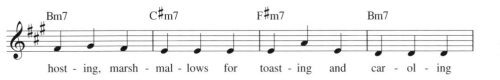

host - ing, marsh - mal - lows for toast - ing and car - ol - ing

out in the snow. There'll be scar - y ghost sto - ries and

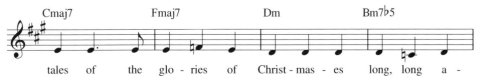

tales of the glo - ries of Christ - mas - es long, long a -

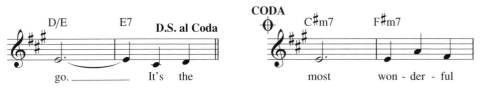

go. _____ It's the most won - der - ful

time _____ of the year. _____

MY FAVORITE THINGS
from THE SOUND OF MUSIC
Lyrics by OSCAR HAMMERSTEIN II
Music by RICHARD RODGERS

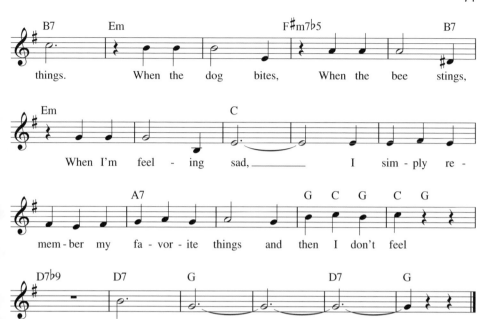

B7	Em		F#m7♭5		B7

things. When the dog bites, When the bee stings,

| Em | | C | | | |

When I'm feel - ing sad, _____ I sim - ply re -

| | A7 | | G C G C G |

mem - ber my fa - vor - ite things and then I don't feel

| D7♭9 | D7 | G | | D7 | G |

so bad. _____

O COME, ALL YE FAITHFUL
(Adeste Fideles)
Words and Music by JOHN FRANCIS WADE
translated by Frederick Oakley

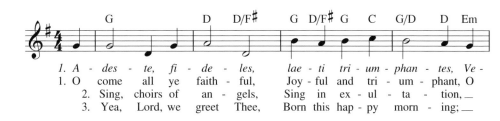

1. A - des - te, fi - de - les, lae - ti tri - um - phan - tes, Ve -
1. O come all ye faith - ful, Joy - ful and tri - um - phant, O
2. Sing, choirs of an - gels, Sing in ex - ul - ta - tion, __
3. Yea, Lord, we greet Thee, Born this hap - py morn - ing; __

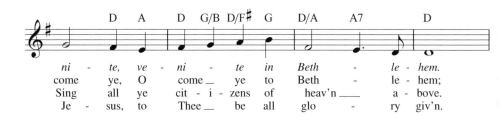

ni - te, ve - ni - te in Beth - le - hem.
come ye, O come __ ye to Beth - le - hem;
Sing all ye cit - i - zens of heav'n ___ a - bove.
Je - sus, to Thee __ be all glo - ry giv'n.

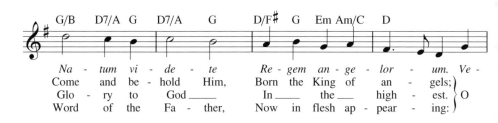

Na - tum vi - de - te Re - gem an - ge - lor - um. Ve -
Come and be - hold Him, Born the King of an - gels;
Glo - ry to God ___ In ___ the __ high - est. O
Word of the Fa - ther, Now in flesh ap - pear - ing:

ni - te a - do - re - mus, ve - ni - te a - do - re - mus, ve -
come let us a - dore Him, O come let us a - dore Him, O

ni - te a - do - re - mus __ Do - mi - num.
come let us a - dore Him, __ Christ ___ the Lord.

O HOLY NIGHT

French Words by PLACIDE CAPPEAU
English Words by JOHN S. DWIGHT
Music by ADOLPHE ADAM

O LITTLE TOWN OF BETHLEHEM

Words by PHILLIPS BROOKS
Music by LEWIS H. REDNER

O lit - tle town of Beth - le - hem, How still we __ see thee
For Christ is born of Mar - y, And gath - ered _ all a -
How si - lent - ly, how si - lent - ly The won - drous gift is
O ho - ly Child of Beth - le - hem, De - scend to __ us, we

lie; A - bove thy deep and dream - less sleep The
bove, While mor - tals sleep, the an - gels keep Their
giv'n! So God im - parts to hu - man hearts The
pray; Cast out our sin and en - ter in; Be

si - lent __ stars go by. Yet in thy dark streets
watch of __ won - d'ring love. O morn - ing stars, to -
bless - ings __ of His heav'n. No ear may hear His
born in __ us to - day. We hear the Christ - mas

shin - eth The ev - er - last - ing light; The hopes and fears of
geth - er Pro - claim the ho - ly birth! And prais - es sing to
com - ing, But in this world of sin, Where meek souls will re -
an - gels The great glad tid - ings tell; O come to us, a -

all the years Are met in thee to - night.
God the King, And peace to men on earth.
ceive Him still, The dear Christ en - ters in.
bide with us, Our Lord Em - man - u - el!

SANTA CLAUS IS COMIN' TO TOWN

Words by HAVEN GILLESPIE
Music by J. FRED COOTS

ROCKIN' AROUND THE CHRISTMAS TREE

Music and Lyrics by
JOHNNY MARKS

Rock in' a - round the Christ-mas tree. _ Have a hap - py hol - i - day. _

_ Ev-'ry-one danc - ing mer - ri - ly _ in the new old fash-ioned

way. new old fash - ioned way. _____

RUDOLPH THE RED-NOSED REINDEER

Music and Lyrics by
JOHNNY MARKS

say, "Ru - dolph, with your nose so bright, won't you guide my

sleigh to - night?" _ Then how the rein - deer loved him

as they shout - ed out with glee: "Ru - dolph the red - nosed rein - deer,

you'll go down in his - to - ry!" _____

SHAKE ME I RATTLE

(Squeeze Me I Cry)

Words and Music by HAL HACKADY
and CHARLES NAYLOR

Moderately slow

I was pass - ing by a toy shop on the cor - ner of the
called an - oth - er toy shop on a square so long a -
late and snow was fall - ing as the shop - pers hur - ried

square, where a lit - tle girl was look - ing in the win - dow
go, where I saw a lit - tle dol - ly that I want - ed
by past the girl - ie at the win - dow with her lit - tle head held

there. She was look - ing at a dol - ly in a dress of ros - y
so. I re - mem - bered, I re - mem - bered how I longed to make it
high. They were clos - ing up the toy shop as I hur - ried thru the

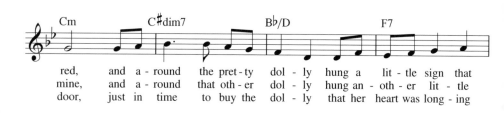

red, and a - round the pret - ty dol - ly hung a lit - tle sign that
mine, and a - round that oth - er dol - ly hung an - oth - er lit - tle
door, just in time to buy the dol - ly that her heart was long - ing

said:
sign: Shake me, I rat - tle. Squeeze me, I
for.

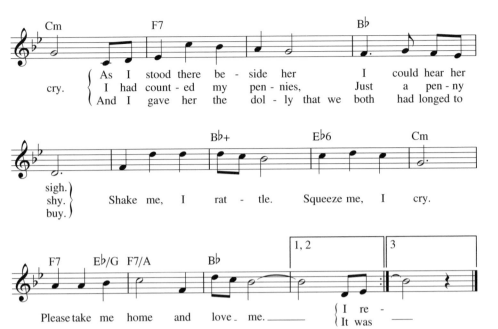

Cm   **F7**   **B♭**

cry.

As I stood there be - side her   I   could hear her
I had count - ed my pen - nies,   Just   a   pen - ny
And I gave her the dol - ly that we both had longed to

B♭+   **E♭6**   **Cm**

sigh.
shy.   Shake me, I rat - tle. Squeeze me, I cry.
buy.

F7   **E♭/G**   **F7/A**   **B♭**

1, 2   **3**

Please take me home and love_ me._____

I re -
It was _____

SILENT NIGHT

Words by JOSEPH MOHR
Translated by JOHN F. YOUNG
Music by FRANZ X. GRUBER

SILVER BELLS

from the Paramount Picture THE LEMON DROP KID
Words and Music by JAY LIVINGSTON
and RAY EVANS

SOMEWHERE IN MY MEMORY

from the Twentieth Century Fox Motion Picture HOME ALONE
Words by LESLIE BRICUSSE
Music by JOHN WILLIAMS

THIS CHRISTMAS

Words and Music by DONNY HATHAWAY
and NADINE McKINNOR

TOYLAND

from BABES IN TOYLAND

Words by GLEN MacDONOUGH
Music by VICTOR HERBERT

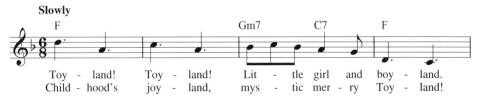

Toy - land! Toy - land! Lit - tle girl and boy - land.
Child - hood's joy - land, mys - tic mer - ry Toy - land!

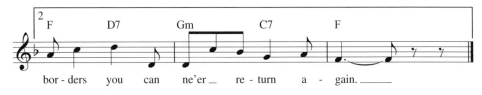

While you dwell with - in it ____ you are ev - er hap - py then.
Once you pass its

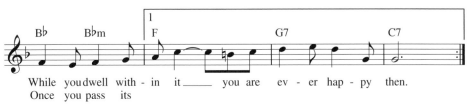

bor - ders you can ne'er __ re - turn a - gain. ____

UP ON THE HOUSETOP

Words and Music by
B.R. HANDY

Brightly

Up on the house - top __ rein - deer pause, Out jumps good old
First comes the stock - ing of lit - tle Nell; Oh, dear San - ta,
Next comes the stock - ing of lit - tle Will; Oh, just see what a

San - ta Claus; Down thro' the chim - ney with lots of toys,
fill it well; Give her a dol - lie that laughs and cries,
glo - rious fill! Here is a ham - mer and lots of tacks,

All for the lit - tle ones, Christ - mas joys.
One that will o - pen and shut her eyes. Ho, ho, ho!
Al - so a ball and a whip that cracks.

who would-n't go! Ho, ho, ho! who would-n't go! __ Up on the house- top,

click, click, click. Down thro' the chim-ney with good Saint Nick.

THE TWELVE DAYS OF CHRISTMAS

Traditional English Carol

Six geese a - lay - ing, Five gold - en rings!

Four _ call - ing birds, Three French hens, Two _ tur - tle doves, And a

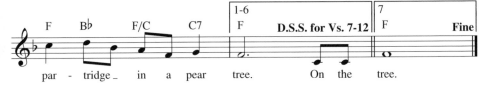

par - tridge _ in a pear tree. On the tree.

7. On the seventh day of Christmas my true love gave to me:
    Seven swans a-swimming,…

8. …Eight maids a-milking,…

9. …Nine ladies dancing,…

10. …Ten lords a-leaping,…

11. …'Leven pipers piping,…

12. …Twelve drummers drumming,…

WE THREE KINGS OF ORIENT ARE

Words and Music by
JOHN H. HOPKINS, JR.

WE WISH YOU A MERRY CHRISTMAS

Traditional English Folksong

Gaily C   F   D7

We wish you a mer-ry Christ-mas, we wish you a mer-ry

G7   E7   Am   F   G7

Christ-mas, we wish you a mer-ry Christ-mas, And a hap-py New

C   Am   Em   D7   G

Year! Good tid-ings to you, wher-ev-er you are; Good

C   G   D7   G7   C

tid-ings for Christ-mas, And a hap-py New Year!

WHAT ARE YOU DOING NEW YEAR'S EVE?

By FRANK LOESSER

Slowly and sentimentally

When the bells all ring, _____ and the horns all blow, _____ And the cou-ples we know _____ are fond-ly kiss - ing, _____ Will I be with you, _____ or will I be a-mong the miss - ing? _____

May-be it's much too ear - ly in the game, _
Won-der whose arms will hold you good and tight, _

Ah, but I thought I'd ask you just the same, _
When it's ex - act - ly twelve 'o - clock that night. _

what are you do - ing) new year's, New Year's
Wel-com-ing in the)

Eve? New Year's Eve.

Am		D7	Fm	Bb9	Am	

May be I'm cra - zy   to   sup - pose   I'd ev - er be the

Bm7b5	Bb9	Am	F#m7b5	Fmaj7	D9

one   you   chose   out of the thou-sand   in - vi - ta - tions

G7	G9	C7	F#dim	C7	F

you'll   re   -   ceive.   Ah, but in case I

Eb7		F

stand   one lit - tle   chance, _   Here comes the jack - pot

Bb	Bbm	F	Dm7

ques - tion in   ad - vance: _   What are you do - ing

G7	C9	Gm9	C7b9	F	Bb	F

new   year's,   New   Year's   Eve?

WONDERFUL CHRISTMASTIME

Words and Music by
PAUL McCARTNEY

Brightly

Bb   Bbmaj7   Bb

The mood is   right, ___   the spir - it's   up, ___
The par - ty's   on ___   the feel - ing's   here ___
The word is   out ___   a - bout the   town, ___

Gm/Bb   Bb   F/Bb

___   we're here   to - night ___
___   that on - ly   comes ___
___   to lift   a   glass, ___

Bb   Cm7   Cm7/F

and that's   e - nough. ___
this time   of   year. ___
oh don't   look   down. ___   Sim - ply

Dm   Dm/G   Eb   Ab9   Bb   Cm7   Cm7/F

hav - ing   a   won - der-ful Christ - mas - time.   Sim - ply

Dm   Dm/G   Eb   Ab9   1. Bb   2, 3 Bb

hav - ing   a   won - der-ful Christ - mas - time.   time.

Gm   Cm7   F7   Bb

The   choir   of   chil - dren   sing   their   song. (They
(2nd time only)

To Coda ⊕

Gm   Cm7   F7   Bb

prac - tised   all   year   long.)   Ding   dong, ding

Eb   Cm7

dong. Ding   dong, ding.   Ooh ___   Ooh ___

YOU'RE ALL I WANT FOR CHRISTMAS

Words and Music by GLEN MOORE
and SEGER ELLIS